America
Border
Culture
Dreamer

THE YOUNG IMMIGRANT EXPERIENCE
FROM A TO Z

WENDY EWALD

Little, Brown and Company
New York Boston

A Note from the Author

Why the alphabet? Like most everyone, I first encountered written language in children's alphabet primers. I see now that the words and visual examples used to represent letters reinforced the worldview of the middle-class white girl I happened to be. The letter *C*, for example, was illustrated by a picture of a shiny new car.

With this in mind, I started using alphabets with photographs to teach language to ESOL (English for Speakers of Other Languages) students. With their help, I made pictures with them to illustrate the alphabet so children could influence the images and meaning of a primer—in effect, make it their own.

Beyond that, I realized the alphabet could be an effective tool to pick apart and document something as inexpressible as the experience of immigration. In a time of turmoil and confusion and fear, I thought it was important for young immigrants to tell their own story in a form that was playful and understandable for an American audience.

When Al-Bustan Seeds of Culture, an arts and education organization in Philadelphia, commissioned me to work with high school teens in creating a public installation, I proposed *An Immigrant Alphabet*. Eighteen students from Northeast High School whose families had immigrated to the US volunteered to work with us. The first step was to discuss and research immigration as it was evolving each day and to share their stories with each other.

We divided the alphabet into parts and assigned students to groups to choose words to represent their letters. Then the students drew out their photographic ideas. The third stage was to create a studio in the courtyard of the school where we, the students and I, set up the shots, and I photographed them. Then the students added the letters and words represented in English and their native language. All art appears precisely as the students individually created it, meaning the styles vary from letter to letter.

Finally, I asked the students to come up with questions they'd like to ask each other. I used the questions to interview each of them. In these interviews the teenagers discuss what it takes to leave their country and what it takes to survive in the unknown world of the US. I was amazed by their curiosity and compassion for each other.

Xuan from Vietnam told me:

> *The stories that are heard here, they came from countries where the students wouldn't be able to go to school and make friends and have the life that they're enjoying now. It's so easy to let our emotions guide us and sometimes block the difficulties away and say that it doesn't matter because that doesn't affect me. But if you keep thinking like that eventually then you're going to get hurt too. We came from countries where the people also thought that what happens in other places doesn't affect me until it was too late.*

Why did I like this project? It helped me think about a good future for our country. There are hundreds of thousands of young immigrants across this country and others. This book portrays just one group of immigrants in one high school in one city, but their experiences of moving and starting life over have been experienced by many of us in our lives, especially as adolescents who are in the midst of forming their identities. I hope this book will inspire others to understand and reach out to immigrants in their communities.

–Wendy

America: Amerika (Uzbek) n. a country where everything starts first

I'm grateful to be in America. There is so much to see, but it's not easy to move in a foreign country where everything is new—friends, school, language, people, food, and places.

Malika, Uzbekistan

In 2011, on September 2, it was the first day of school in my country. We actually won a green card in the lottery. My aunt had persuaded us to apply. It was like a dream for us. America—*what?* Even though I never thought I would come to the USA, every night when I went to bed I would pray, because my best friend came to the USA and she got a green card.

We used to live together in our country. Our houses had connecting roofs and they weren't too tall. We would be playing loud all the time, so from the roof we would go to each other's house.

It was really hard for me to lose my friend because we grew up together. But after she came back from America, she changed. She talked to me with English words I didn't understand.

The immigration officers came to our house, but they didn't tell us anything at first. They said we're looking for your dad, not you or your mother. We thought something violent had happened. They were talking so serious, and they didn't show their emotions.

They went to where my dad worked and told him he had won a green card. In the beginning he wouldn't go along. But my mom was like, "No, this is for the kids, not for me. I want to see the kids educated and working in good places as professionals. What am I for in this life if I don't see that?" My grandmother persuaded my dad because education is really expensive in my country.

It was the last day of school—May 25, 2012. I was twelve years old. My mom, my dad, me—we all came here together by plane from Tashkent, the capital city of Uzbekistan. When I got off the plane, I was looking all around, opening my eyes, opening my mouth. I'd never seen this stuff in my life. I'd never seen African American people.

In the beginning my health wasn't good because of the weather. I slept all day, all night. I couldn't wake up; I had asthma and I had to sleep on a couch.

I thought about how I used to sleep and play in my country. We didn't have a really good life there, but I was happy inside. Here, at first we lived in a town that was really quiet. I didn't have any friends. All the kids did was watch TV, TV, TV, TV. I would ask my parents to send me back to Uzbekistan because I thought the things would never change.

In America, education is good. If you study hard, you can become someone. I'm grateful that I came because I wouldn't be the same person I am right now; I would still be thinking in little ways.

America changed me so much. It gave me a hope to a better and amazing life that I have dreamed of all the time. I want to do something that people will remember. I want to study business and help people in other countries.

In a small way, I think that we can change something in someone's life in a good way.

Bien giới

BORDER

13,b

Border: Biên giới (Vietnamese) n. an imaginary line separating countries and people

We cross the border for the sole purpose of protecting our families and to live a fuller life.

Culture: ثقافة (Arabic) n. the customs, art, and achievements of a particular country

Brides use henna to make themselves more beautiful for their weddings since it is part of their culture.

Mariam, Egypt

We came here to Philadelphia in April at twelve o'clock at night. It was cold, not our weather. I was wearing my mom's jacket but it didn't help. I told her, "I'm cold, I want to go back."

When you see the buildings here, it's like you cannot hear any voices. It's so quiet, so quiet. You feel like the people in the houses are dead. In our country, when you walk outside you can hear voices or noise from anywhere. You would be like, I have a headache. I don't like to walk in the street when you cannot hear like the clacks of the cars. Why is it so quiet? The buildings, the schools, the church, even the church. Why is it so quiet?

———

When I first got here, I was like, oh, new stuff. America is awesome. Then my aunt asked me if I wanted to see the school. OK, I thought, I'm going to see blondie girls and blondie boys and be like, ooooh. But when I came, I first saw African American people. I was like, OK, they're American so…Then I saw an Arab, I saw an Indian, I saw Chinese people and others from around the whole world! I was like, huh, where am I? I said I'm going back. I'm going to get a taxi, I'm going back. I cannot stay here. It's all Arab. I'm not in America. I'm in my country. I just traveled to another city.

I thought in America I'm going to be the only one in the street wearing a dress. But it's normal. I eat the same food. I see Arabs, I see Egyptians. The whole school, everywhere I go. Every corner there is an Egyptian. I thought I'd be the only Muslim in America, the only Arabic girl in America. I was going to be the only girl who left their country and came to America.

———

America was a movie to me, but we are all immigrants here. No one is better than another one. We are equal. We are all immigrants. When we came here, we were allowed to do anything. Anywhere, whenever you want to do something, you can do it. But in our country, we're not allowed to. We cannot shake hands with a boy. If you look at the Qur'an and read it, it's haram [forbidden]. But people came here and started to hug girls, and kiss them. It's OK if you hug a girl, but not in the street, or in the school.

I'm trying to stay as I am. It's Mariam, I came here. I didn't change. We have habits in our country. I can hug most of my friends, but when I have a boyfriend, it's different. He's not going to marry me so why I'm walking with him in the hallways and holding hands.

Here we live with one hand, me and my mom, as if we were one person. I cannot leave her because my dad is not here. She started working when we came from Egypt. I was like, no, Mom, you cannot work. I was thinking to leave the school and work for her. She told me no, so I take care of my little brother. And he was like, "Where's my mom? Why she works?" One night, I saw her crying. "What happened?" She told me we need money to pay for the rent and the food. I said, "Let's go back to our country." She said, "No, we will not give up."

Dreamer: Soñador (Spanish) n. a child brought to a different country illegally, often without having control or giving an opinion

To be a DREAMer is to be isolated at a young age.

George, Argentina

A DREAMer is a person like me. I was only ten months old when my family made the choice. I wasn't old enough to say no; I wanted to stay in Argentina. But my parents did the right thing.

We're called DREAMers 'cause we're dreaming of making a future for ourselves and our growing families. It means we want to go to college, we want to do what our parents weren't able to do, and we want to do what our parents came here for: to get a good education and jobs.

I don't consider myself an immigrant, but that's the label the US puts on me. If people would listen, they would realize I was raised here, had my education here. This is where I'm from. If we had the chance to speak out, if all the DREAMers were to show up on one day and say what's on our mind, I think it would change a lot of opinions. We all have a different story. The main thing is, we were raised here.

I first realized I was an immigrant when I started doing all the paperwork. This happens at the age of fourteen, when you can first apply to be a DREAMer. I always knew about it but my parents let me live my life happy; they didn't want me to have that worry in my head all the time.

But there's always the what-if factor.

What if one day I get in trouble and it's not my fault? Things can escalate very badly. And I worry about having parents that are also wanting to be legal and running the risk of them getting in trouble by accident. Then it's, you know, pack your bags and leave. Like what if tomorrow I wake up, and I'm not in the US anymore or I'm on a plane going back? I don't want to ask my parents too much because it gets them thinking, and it gets them upset. I feel like if they were to get in trouble…well, we're old enough to handle it.

We had no family in the US. We left family and friends back there. Now we can't see them because Argentina's too far away.

I only want to go back to visit, see family I've never seen. They're my family; they'll always be my family. I just want to know, to see where I was born and where I was supposed to be raised. But I choose to stay in the US. The US is good. It's treated my family well.

Education: Ta'lim (Uzbek) n. a power that no one can take away

Education is not only being in school, but also learning from the life around me.

Faith: Dức Tin (Vietnamese) n. a strong trust and confidence in one's religion or trust in another person

I have faith in God's plan for me and that he will protect me from danger on my journey.

Xuan, Vietnam

My dad and mom had to live through the devastation after the war. My dad had to go fishing for frogs and fish and other small animals to feed the family.

My mom always tried to motivate me to work hard and not take my life for granted. She drove the point home often by telling me about how her family used to live a very poor life in Vietnam. She liked to find scraps of clothes and use her mother's friend's sewing machine to make her own clothes to wear. She and my grandmother would make a living from selling fabric, soy milk, and sweet rice on the street. It makes me sad sometimes. If she didn't have to work in a nail salon and move to America for her children, would she be a different person? Maybe she could have had a career in designing and making fashion since it seemed to me that was her dream.

I do miss my family in Vietnam even though I don't remember some of their faces. My mom never really shows me pictures of them. If I were to look at them now I wouldn't recognize their faces. I kind of want to go back, but when I came to America I left that part of me back there. I was just learning English.

For first grade, a girl named Gabriella lived close to me and we would wait at the bus stop together. She'd always try and talk to me. I remember one conversation we had, even though I didn't know the language. One day on the bus coming home from school she was talking to me about magazines she had about George Washington, myths about him, and an article about how dogs can't eat chocolate. She kept asking me questions. All I could say was yes and no randomly because I didn't know how to talk to her.

I still know Vietnamese because I talk to my parents in Vietnamese, but even though I have Vietnamese friends here they don't like speaking Vietnamese. We try but we end up talking in English again. In Vietnam I also had education in learning Chinese because my dad was also Chinese. Moving to America I lost that opportunity, so I only know two languages now. I'm hoping to eventually get the chance to talk with my dad and ask him to teach me.

I was in seventh grade when we finally were able to get our citizenship. This became my new home. I gained a new identity. I feel like I was on a long trip through Vietnam and then I came home. We had to go to city hall and into a room where I saw a lot of people who I didn't know. Everyone had to take an oath. Afterwards we became citizens! But you're obligated to make that oath whereas I'm sure that if I were to ask my friends who were native-born in America they wouldn't know it.

I don't think anyone should think that all an immigrant is doing is moving. My country had very tight governmental control and the society was very poor. How are you going to raise your children in that? In America, where you have countless accounts and histories of people discriminating against each other, we shouldn't be having this problem now.

Gg Green Card

Tarjeta Verde

Green Card: Tarjeta Verde (Spanish) n. a piece of plastic that allows you to move freely across the US

My brother Paul has to carry his green card everywhere because of his daily attire and skin color.

Joseph, Dominican Republic and El Salvador

A green card is slang for a residency card. You have to renew it every ten years until you become a citizen. After a while it expires, so it's like having a temporary license to live here. Once you're a resident of your state you can apply for citizenship and then take the test. I'm mixed. My mom is from the Dominican Republic and my dad is from El Salvador. They're two completely different cultures. They're both in me, I guess.

My dad came here in the mid-eighties. I've seen some photos of him when he arrived. He actually drove all the way twice, because he got sent back, but now he's a resident here. I remember my dad studying for the citizenship test. He had it on an iPod. Once you pass the test, you can apply for government jobs.

My mom came here legally in the late eighties, early nineties, right before she turned into an adult. The US has the most strict immigration process. It takes years of background checks. They're not just checking you, they're checking your distant relatives for the littlest thing that anyone did in the past.

Why does anyone want to come to the US? To find a better life. El Salvador is extremely poor. Now, here in Pennsylvania, my mom is a home health aide nurse and my dad works in a cardboard box company with my cousin. They do all the packaging for Hershey. So if you ever see a cardboard box with Hershey written on it, you know it's my dad's company.

I've been to El Salvador. I was still young. I thought the world was safe there; I was with my family. But years later I understand bad stuff does happen there. Now as I think about going back, I have to be more cautious, especially since I'm a teenager turning into an adult. I don't really see myself ever living there. It's very bad because of gangs, especially in San Salvador or Santa Anna—there's a lot of violence. The gang members overpopulate the prisons there. There's more of them than cops.

I feel there's a misunderstanding of immigrants. They see us as bad people. People say if you want to come to this country, do it legally. Yes, we can do it legally, but they have to understand that sometimes that takes too long, we can't wait. When people come in the illegal way it's because that's their only way of doing it. Think about all the Syrian families trying to come here and all the refugees. Each person has a different story.

Happiness: আনন্দ (Bengali) n. the explosion of joy one feels within oneself when one's heart is full

I feel a burst of happiness when I explore the big city of Philadelphia.

Tania, Bangladesh

I came from Bangladesh when I was thirteen. We got our visas seven years after we were accepted. My mom kept saying, we're going to go to the US, and me and my sister would laugh. We're never going to get there, we thought, it's never going to happen.

Then one day we got a call from the embassy. I was too childish to understand what was happening. I didn't realize I was going to leave my older sister. I curled up in the corner of my room and cried. My sister kept saying, "You guys are going to come and visit us, and we'll come there." I called her from the airport. "Can you just come and pick me up?" I said. "I don't want to go!" She kept telling me, "You're so happy, you're not even going to miss me." I was slouched in the chair and crying out loud. "Can I go home? I don't want to be here!" Everybody was looking at me.

Sometimes I feel like life just changed, my whole life. When I first came I was just a scaredy girl, and I didn't like to go out with my friends. Now I'm not scared to talk to anyone in English. Now I feel like it's my house, like it's Bangladesh, it's the same thing for me now. It's nice here, I like it. I did go back to my country again in summer for three months for my brothers' weddings. And when I was there, I was missing my friends here. And the big thing was: the Wi-Fi—I missed my Wi-Fi connection!

When we moved here, we used to wear our Bengali clothes when we went out, and everyone looked at us like we were different, and we looked at ourselves like we were different. We wanted to wear American clothes. When I'm at home I wear traditional clothes. I feel comfortable wearing our traditional clothes. They're so soft and nice.

Last year sometimes I wore a hijab in class. Nobody looked at me or talked to me, so I kept really quiet. This year I'm not wearing my hijab and some people who didn't even look at me last year come over to me and talk. They don't even realize I had class with them last year. Even some of my teachers don't. I feel kind of fake because I want to wear the hijab but I feel like if I wear it, I'll be different from my friends.

A relative in Philadelphia told my dad, "You should look after your daughters, they're putting out American vibes." My dad said, "I trust my daughters not to do bad things. I taught them how to live free, and they should enjoy it here." My dad tells us, "Be careful. If you need help call me." That's it.

My dad is so worried about us because of everything that's happening. I tell my dad like, look, I trust America. I came legally and I didn't do anything wrong, they're not going to send me back. I trust America.

Ii

Immigrant

Immigrant

Immigrant: Immigrant (Uzbek) n. someone who migrates from one country to another to start a new page of their life

I like being an immigrant. I have a chance to meet different people in my life and learn something new about their culture. It's fascinating and gives me an opportunity to shape my life differently.

Jewelry: গয়না (Bengali) n. articles of gold, silver, precious stones for personal adornment

My mother brought her jewelry with her because it reminded her of her past, her family and traditions.

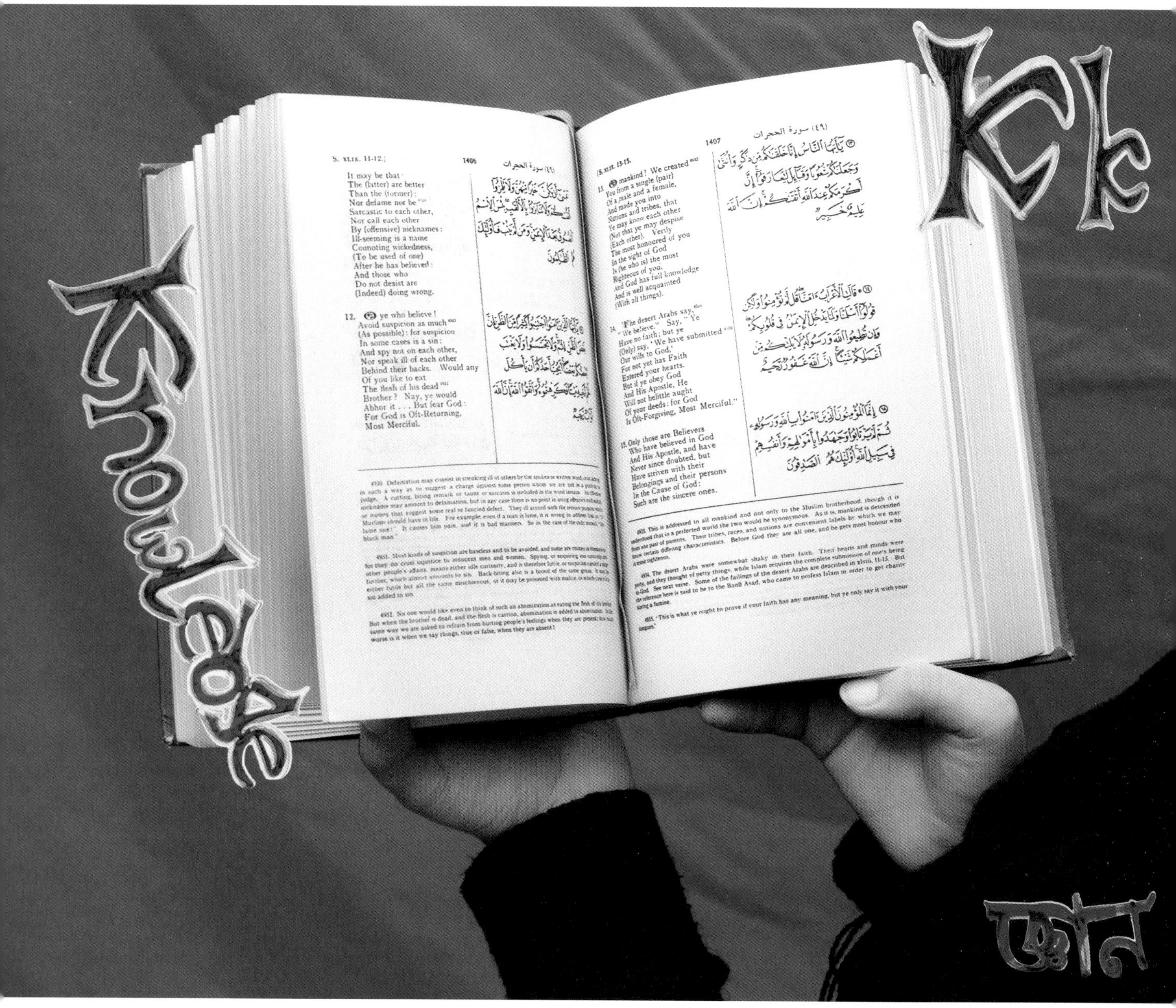

Knowledge
S. XLIX. 11-12.
1406
It may be that
The (latter) are better
Than the (former):
Nor defame nor be
Sarcastic to each other,
Nor call each other
By (offensive) nicknames:
Ill-seeming is a name
Connoting wickedness,
(To be used of one)
After he has believed:
And those who
Do not desist are
(Indeed) doing wrong.
12. O ye who believe!
Avoid suspicion as much
(As possible): for suspicion
In some cases is a sin:
And spy not on each other,
Nor speak ill of each other
Behind their backs. Would any
Of you like to eat
The flesh of his dead
Brother? Nay, ye would
Abhor it . . . But fear God:
For God is Oft-Returning,
Most Merciful.
S. XLIX. 13-15.
1407
13. O mankind! We created
You from a single (pair)
Of a male and a female,
And made you into
Nations and tribes, that
Ye may know each other
(Not that ye may despise
Each other). Verily
The most honoured of you
In the sight of God
Is (he who is) the most
Righteous of you.
And God has full knowledge
And is well acquainted
(With all things).
14. The desert Arabs say,
"We believe." Say, "Ye
Have no faith; but ye
(Only) say, 'We have submitted
Our wills to God,'
For not yet has Faith
Entered your hearts.
But if ye obey God
And His Apostle, He
Will not belittle aught
Of your deeds: for God
Is Oft-Forgiving, Most Merciful."
15. Only those are Believers
Who have believed in God
And His Apostle, and have
Never since doubted, but
Have striven with their
Belongings and their persons
In the Cause of God:
Such are the sincere ones.

Knowledge: জ্ঞান (Bengali) n. the sum of what is known

I think my faith is a good source of knowledge. It helps me stay on track.

Kazi, Bangladesh

My first thought was, I'm going to America. It's going to be different. In our country you always live with fear. In America I thought the roads were going to be different. It's going to be cleaner, you can go anywhere freely. But it's not like that. I thought it was going to be like the movies but it's almost like how it was in my country. You can go anywhere by yourself, but you know, you still have that fear, like what's going to happen to you if you go out by yourself at ten o'clock. You don't know if you can walk there, and there's like other kinds of people.

We were living in Habiganj. We rented a car and then hired a driver who drove us to Dhaka. And we stayed in my aunt's house. My aunt applied for us to come to the US.

It was my first time going in a plane. I thought we would go up by the stairs and see the plane above us. But it was a room you walk through. We flew to Dubai. Then we went from Dubai to New York where my family was waiting for us.

We all came at the same time, me, my dad, my brother, my mom, and my aunt. We flew on Christmas and there were decorations outside.

From there, we came here to Philadelphia. When I got to the house I took a shower. I couldn't get my eyes open. They just closed by themselves. I woke up in the morning, six something. It's eleven hours difference from here to our country, so for the first month I woke up so early.

All of my dad's relatives and my uncles and aunts were together for two weeks. So we were busy talking with each other and going out.

I came from one country, then started a new life. I didn't feel strange. Not really. I could see the difference in the clothing people wear. The day I started school I started wearing the hijab. It feels weird when you just start doing it but I'd decided and it was cold outside too. It became a habit. It was the right time to start wearing it. But it was my culture too.

My dad works at Marshalls. My mom works at Burger King. I work at Burger King too. I have a part-time job. I take the order, take the money, then give the food to the customer. I won the award for Employee of the Month. People are nice to me. And I didn't want to keep asking my parents for money.

The difference between other kids and immigrants is some of us feel alone. Some of us miss our country a lot. I miss the food because it was all halal. You could go to almost any store and get something. Here you have to look for halal. I miss my country too, but not as much as some of the kids I talk to. They want to go back so bad.

I was happy there. I'm still happy here. I'm happy.

Ll Leave

Terk etmek

Leave: Terk etmek (Turkish) v. to go away from somewhere or someone
When I was leaving Turkey, I could not breathe. It was like I was dying.

Rushana, Tajikistan/Turkey

I'm from Tajikistan, but when people ask, I say I'm from Turkey, because I'm a refugee. My mom was a journalist who was writing the true facts about human rights in Tajikistan, about education, and about the dirty stuff our government was doing in other countries.

This corruption started after the Soviet Union broke up and Tajikistan became independent. Russia was helping our president. Now he's president for life. The Tajik government sold our resources—minerals and oil to Russia, China, and other countries—but in Tajikistan there were a lot of people who were earning $100 a month. Is that enough for a government job? Any job?

My dad was working for our president. He was like an aide, supporting and taking care of the president. The problem was the government didn't like what my mom was writing. "Who are you, writing about us? You're a Turk. You're not allowed to write that."

My mom just said, "It is my job. I'm not supporting any side. I'm not making fake news." She was working in Radio Liberty. That's American radio in Tajikistan.

We had everything in Tajikistan—car, house, clothes. No secondhand stuff. But one night, the government guys called my mom and said, "If you don't stop writing about the government, your kids are not coming home from school. We know where they're taking classes."

They also called my father and said, "You gotta stop your wife or we're gonna kill her, and you too." After that, my father fled to Russia without us.

My mom called some journalists and they told us Turkey was a good country to go to. It was an Islamic country. People were friendly. They bought us tickets.

My mom is Turkish but she was born in Tajikistan. When we got to Turkey, her journalist friends said, "Oh—you're alive?" Everybody thought that they'd killed us, because when we were escaping, we didn't use phones or the Internet and we dropped completely out of touch.

Istanbul was my dream. I was so happy but then I was afraid—what am I going to do? I didn't know the language. People talking, talking, talking around me but what was going on?

While we were in Tajikistan my mom wouldn't wear a scarf. I thought that people wearing scarves were terrorists, even though I'm Muslim. The Tajik community said, "If you believe in Islam, you'll be punished."

In Turkey I learned what Islam actually is. That's where I started to learn the Qur'an, and I said, Islam is not about killing people; Islam actually is peace. God says, "Don't kill. You don't have a right to kill the people or things that I give life." And I said, "All right, this is what the real Islam is."

I loved Turkey because the Turkish people and even the Turkish government supported us and gave us hope. I felt alive then, and I felt we could start from scratch and be successful.

Sometimes I felt ashamed because we had refugee status and people were helping us with money. I'm like, "Mom, I'm not homeless, don't take the money." And my mom said, "They're doing this because they believe in God, they're trying to do good stuff."

My mom's friend from Uzbekistan helped us rent a house. It was very nice, close to the sea. For two months we used the money the journalists gave us.

Then we went to the Turkish government and explained our situation and after a while they sent us to Ankara for an interview. There were four of us kids. The youngest was four and I was the oldest. I was trying to keep my mouth shut and keep everybody happy. My mom was looking at us and crying. We could see all the other refugees from all the different places, like from Syria. We were not so important, because we were just political refugees. There was no war in Tajikistan.

Then they told us that the American government accepted us; we could go to America. We'd be safe there and the Americans would take care of us. They'd give us free food and free clothes. But they also told us, "You can't work because you're refugees."

All right—we took the refugee status and we were actually happy because we were going to America. In America we have everything—water, gas. But in Tajikistan, in winter you don't have electricity. In summer, you don't have water. Why not? Because the Tajikistan government is selling these things to Afghanistan and other countries.

I decided to become a journalist so I could fight against people who discriminated, against the teachers and students and everybody who treated immigrants and refugees unfairly. Whenever I felt the urge, I started writing an article.

Still when we got to America I missed Turkey and I cried a lot for a whole year. I learned one thing: not to trust people before knowing who they are. I learned a lot of other stuff in America, too. I learned how to be tough. I wasn't very tough, not even in Turkey. You come here, you meet people from your own country—from Tajikistan or Russia. They tend to look down on you and give you a hard time.

But I found some friends and they gave me a job in their furniture store. If anybody found out, my boss would be in trouble. He gave me a job anyway.

America is a safer place, because when you become a citizen, if somebody does anything, even if you're a refugee or an immigrant, the government takes care of you, and if somebody's going to do something to you, the government can punish them.

So I feel safe because my family is safe. I don't care about my own life, because I'm not afraid. Before, I was afraid of somebody doing something to my mom, and how am I going to take care of these three kids, because I'm too young and I don't have the experience that Mom has. And of course, my sisters and brothers, they don't have enough experience to defend themselves, and they don't know enough English. I would have to take care of them.

I really wanted to be a soccer player when I came here. The coach said, "You're too old to play on this team." I said, "But I came to America so my family would be safe and I could play soccer here. And everybody has a right to do whatever they want to." They said, "Sorry, we can't take you." I felt so hopeless. I didn't see soccer as a hobby, soccer was who I was.

I decided to become a journalist so I could fight against people who discriminated, against the teachers and students and everybody who treated immigrants and refugees unfairly. Whenever I felt the urge, I started writing an article.

When my mom read my articles, she said, "This is so emotional. It's not journalism. You can't take one side. You should be in the middle. It's a good start, but you have a lot to learn."

Memory

MM

Memory: ذكريات (Arabic) n. something that you remember from the country where you were born

All my good memories are from Sudan.

Salawat, Sudan

First, immigrants work harder than the others. If this country didn't have immigrants, I don't know how it would be.

I lived in Sudan and I saw a million people die because they didn't have food. They didn't have a home, and they didn't go to the hospital because they didn't have money to pay to the doctor. Even in the city I lived in, Khartoum, a lot of people died. There is no free doctor there.

I told my mom, when I was little, "If God lets me go to America and be a doctor, I'll come back and build a big hospital that's free for everyone. It's not a reason to die—that you don't have money." In Sudan, if you want to become a doctor it takes four years. And here they say it's gonna take me ten years. I have a lot of dreams.

Here in America they give out numbers to the poor countries like Sudan and Egypt, like it is a game you play. You have to go and apply to come to America. Then in America they pick the numbers, and then after six months, they'll call and tell you if you win or not.

My dad's a teacher. He worked regular hours from seven until four and after school he tutored students at our house. He couldn't afford the tickets to America. My mom sold stuff from our house, her gold and everything. We rented the house, the TV, everything.

I came with my dad and my mom and my three brothers and four sisters. I left my family there, and I'm not sure when I'm going to see them. We don't know who is gonna live and who is gonna die.

I have an aunt here, but she's not really an aunt. She's from my dad's country. We stayed at her house at first. This is not the America that I imagined. It's worse than Sudan, in some places. Every day the police came because someone had shot someone else. And I didn't think a school would have bad people, people that bully you. I'm older, but I worry about my little sister and brother.

But I'm thankful that I came. I was in danger sometimes at school. If it rains too much, the mud houses collapse and they have to close the school. A million people in Sudan don't have the things that I have, the school that I go to, the house that I live in, the food that I eat. I came here for one thing: to study and finish college and get myself educated. I wanna work here first so I can build a free hospital in Sudan.

I will never give up in this life. I will protect my family. I will give my dad and my mom the things that they gave me, and make them proud of me. And for my other family members, I'll let them know that I left because of one reason: to study and become someone in this life.

Now: Ahora (Spanish) adj. at a present moment

I'm not a friend of procrastination, nor am I patient (waiting to get things done). I like to do things now.

Gabriel, Dominican Republic

Thankfully, I'm an American. My mom and dad were married in Santo Domingo but they got divorced when they were already in the process of coming here to America. My mom got pregnant with me while they were still in Santo Domingo, but after I was born here my mom and I went straight back again to the Dominican Republic.

I spent ten years living in the Dominican Republic. One day my father came to me and showed me my passport. It was a US passport, and I'm like, wow, isn't it supposed to say Dominican? And he said no, son, you are an American, you've always been American.

Later on, after I landed in America, everyone told me, welcome back to your country!

The first school I went to was a big school full of white kids. My mom got me in and of course I didn't know any English. I used to do my assignments with the help of Google Translate! That's the way I survived my whole sixth-grade year. I didn't have help. So it was the toughest year, to be honest. No support. It both pisses me off and kind of makes me happy about myself.

I used to play a lot of video games back in my day, in English but with subtitles in Spanish. That's how I learned to pronounce certain words like *fight, jar,* that were quite complicated. I listened to English music. I used to like to dance to Michael Jackson. The dance moves with the sounds flowing would kind of help me understand what Michael Jackson was singing. My cousin used to give me a lot of songs from rappers like Tupac and Lil Wayne to listen to. He would tell me, bro, this is some other level stuff. Once you learn English you're going to be really tripped out by what this guy is saying.

I had to change my ways—my style, my ambition, even my voice had to change. I used to say things that were not common. People would often look at me as an annoying child and a troublemaker. Even my hair had to change! I had curly hair, buzz-cut hair my whole life. Now see on this side I have curly hair, but on this I always have it straight. It even turned blond a little bit. I like that. It shows my independence. I mean who's the man now, what, yes!

I had to make an image for myself. For me, there was no fate, no ending to my story. If there was an ending, it had to be a good ending. I always thought that things were going to be somehow handed to me. Like oh, I've got to be a doctor like my mom and dad, but I don't think I have the hands for it. So I have to do something more realistic. Perhaps computer engineering.

America is where I first encountered the word *curfew.* People here are like incarcerated in their homes. When I came here, people told me this is the country of more. More water, more food, more people, more cars, more cell phones, just more life. The only people in the DR that are inside are old people, and even they take a chair outside their homes and sit and watch the street and listen to the music.

Occupy: إحتلال (Arabic) v. to occupy another country or someone else's place

Years ago the British occupied Sudan.

Prisoner: Prizonye (Haitian Creole) n. someone who belongs to someone else or is kept temporarily somewhere

When I came to America, I felt like a prisoner because I felt trapped in a place I didn't know much about.

Duvelt, Haiti

I was twelve when I came from Haiti. I was living in a place called Wané with my father, my little brother, and there were like five cousins of mine. I wouldn't say we were living in a mansion but we had a house with ten rooms. My dad owned a school in Haiti, so we weren't living in poor conditions. I liked it.

I lived for a couple of years in the Dominican Republic with my mom. That was more than ten years ago, so I'm not close to her. When you're missing somebody, you have to keep memories of them. But like if you go to your uncle's, or your aunt's, or grandpa's for a little vacation for two weeks, then in two, three years they slip away.

But I still had young siblings in Haiti that were very close to me so it was very sad, leaving my country.

It was May 29, 2011. We got off the airplane late at night so we only saw white lights. It was beautiful, you know—the highways, the tunnels. I woke up that morning and I felt like a newborn. It's a new life, a fresh start.

I'm happy to be here. One thing I want to underline is, I thought things would be a little bit different. They were saying that if you come to America, it's all peaceful, so I didn't think there would be violence. People were just making up stories, making things a little more exciting than it is.

In Haiti people are very helpful to each other. Here people mostly worry about themselves. I'm going to go to work, and I'm going to get home. There if you have a dollar you split it in four ways.

I think I've changed here because I've been interacting with all types of cultures, with different races. It helps me to be a better person.

I think there was a period of time when I felt I had to change to fit in. But then as I grew up, I sort of got more confidence in myself. I started knowing what I like and what I don't like. And then from there, people started appreciating who I was. Some people who don't know me because of the way I dress when they first see me—they think I'm American. But I consider myself Haitian. I use being Haitian to make myself proud.

I see myself as an immigrant, in a positive way. When people think immigrants, they're thinking terrorists. Not everyone thinks like that but, you know, I see myself as a productive and a very thoughtful immigrant. I'm open-minded, I like to exchange ideas that are helpful to the community. I work hard. I show people respect. Immigrants are not what a lot of people are describing them as.

One thing as we're speaking that comes to mind—I think I miss the fun in Haiti and I regret losing the weather, because the weather nine times out of ten is sunny. By six o'clock in the afternoon, the sun goes down and it's chilly. And the food, you know. All these are great natural things.

Qualified: উপযুক্ত (Bengali) adj. having the training to choose the job you want

My mom is a qualified nutritionist in her country, the Dominican Republic, but in America she is looking for a job.

Refugee

Refugiado

Rr

Refugee: Refugiado (Spanish) n. someone who is running away legally or illegally to better themselves or their family

What makes refugees like my mom and dad happy are their things from home like photos of the bush where they grew up.

Gabrielle, St. Lucia, Guyana, India

I'm very independent and strong. If I'd had a more stable childhood, I wouldn't be so tough.

Even though I was born here, I do consider myself an immigrant. I'm not Americanized at all. You might see kids that were born here but their parents weren't; they're just like regular American kids. I'm not like that. I don't eat anything American. When I'm around my family I have a very strong accent. When I'm in school I try to talk American, but I still talk very fast. When I try and slow down, you might hear me stutter, or I might have to completely stop talking and try to rephrase what I said. I used to have so many speech problems. My first language was English but you should hear me sometimes—my coach makes fun of me.

In Guyana they speak English. In St. Lucia they speak patois, which is kind of like Creole. The elders, the grandmothers, the grandfathers speak it. The older people teach it to their kids. Everyone speaks it, but the main language is English. You don't have to know patois, but they still teach it to you. It's a sign of respect. I taught myself and listened to my family, so I know how to speak it well. I know bits and pieces of so many languages. My uncle married a woman that only spoke Spanish, so I had to learn Spanish, like I had to learn patois. I still know who I am. People might not say that's who I am because I was born in America, but if someone asks me, I just say Caribbean and Indian.

Immigration is a big deal in my family. Not just 'cause everyone's an immigrant—it's their whole lifestyle. Even now we'll hear something on the news and we might still get scared. It's how we react to things. My dad should get upset but he doesn't. The ones that take things seriously are the ones that are actually OK. They can live here without worrying about themselves, so they worry about the other people.

We're from St. Lucia and Guyana. My grandfather was from India. His religion was Hinduism. From India he went to St. Lucia. He grew up there with nothing. His life started when he met my grandmother. So then he tried hard to make a living. Three of my aunts were born in St. Lucia. The rest of them were born in Guyana. The economy was good in Guyana, so he became a gold miner there and he got really wealthy. But all along he was struggling with diabetes. Eventually he lost his leg and his eyesight. Before he died he told my grandmother to move back to St. Lucia, where her family was, so she could be comfortable. My mom was a little girl then. Later she went to Connecticut on a student visa and that's where she had me. She didn't finish because I was a premature baby and I was high-maintenance. My mom was working at a couple of stores and going to college to be a certified registered nurse.

My dad was there, sort of. He wasn't always around. If my mom didn't put his name on the Christmas and birthday gifts, I really wouldn't have known he was my dad.

On my dad's side there are six of us. I have one older sister, two older brothers, and two younger sisters. And on my mom's side I have two little brothers and stepkids of her own from my stepdad. There's like eleven of us. I consider all of them blood.

It's just me and my two brothers and my stepdad's kids that live in Philly. My dad lives in Connecticut along with my other siblings. He's been in America for a while. But I don't know how he got here, if he was legal or illegal. I can understand why he left, 'cause they were living in the ghetto.

My mom stayed here on her student visa until it expired. Then she stayed here illegally for maybe twenty-two years. Now she's getting her citizenship. She's kind of scared about it because of the whole Trump situation. My aunt and I are helping her study for the citizenship test.

It's easy to think that people are here legally when they're not. I would hate to see my other aunt deported because she's like a second mom to me; she's the only one that helped my mom out when I was little. So I was shocked to know she wasn't legal. I didn't know what to say. I mean, her son's legal.…

My dad does things he shouldn't, that can get him sent back home. He's been into that since I was born. He's stopped now. But people are still afraid of him and stay friends with him out of loyalty and because of who he is. But they're friends through fear not love.

You don't have to know patois, but they still teach it to you. It's a sign of respect. I taught myself and listened to my family, so I know how to speak it well. I know bits and pieces of so many languages.…I still know who I am.

One summer I went away with my dad. I wasn't comfortable with my mom. I'd been living with him in Connecticut for a couple months when the cops picked him up. All his kids were living with him then, so he was vulnerable. I didn't want my dad to get deported. 'Cause basically he's the one that brings my siblings together. I wanted to stay but I didn't know when he was going to get out. I was eleven. I was getting bullied. I'd gotten into fights. The fights had nothing to do with my dad. There was a lot of drama. It took a toll on me, honestly.

We had to go to a couple of court dates. The immigration lawyer wrote a letter to the judge saying that I got into a fight because I couldn't function without my dad—basically showing that if he got deported the kids wouldn't be OK. Which made it look like I didn't know why my dad was in jail. On my own I was always a tough cookie. I didn't need anyone to back me up. Eventually my mom came and got me. Two days later my dad got out.

Since my dad's an immigrant, they didn't put him in a regular jail, they took him straight to an immigration jail. That means there's two things that can happen—you get deported or you stay in America. My dad wanted to stay and win his case. That's why we had the immigration lawyer. My dad got freed 'cause they didn't have enough evidence against him to deport him.

When my mom came down to get me, I told her I wasn't going to move back with her. I lived with my aunt for about three years. It was actually really good. I went to a private school and I got involved in choir and basketball.

My parents put a lot of pressure on me because I'm smart. They said, you could do this, you can do that. But you know you're black, you're African American, you're a minority, so it'll be hard for you to get there. But I can achieve just as much as any other person out here and way better.

My mom was always asking me, when are you coming back? I'd say, when you get legal, when you get a job, when you get stable. Now she has a steady government job and she's getting legal. So I began staying with her because of my little brother who was three. I didn't want him to grow up without me. He just knew he had a sister named Gabby but he couldn't put a face on it. Or my other little brother, I grew up with him from the time he was born. So I'm basically here for them, no matter what the problems might be.

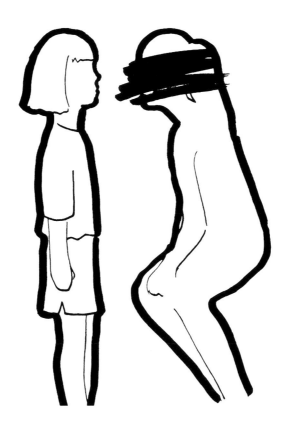

S,s

STEREOTYPE

刻板印象

Stereotype: 刻板印象 (Chinese) n. assumptions about certain types of people because of their characteristics

To me, a stereotype is the same as an uneducated guess. We subconsciously stereotype different people. People stereotype me, too.

Jenny, China

People assume that my nationality is Chinese. My parents are Chinese. But I'm an American. I was born here, and American culture is what I know best.

My grandfather was a sailor and he came here on a ship. He didn't agree with the Communist government, even though it made a lot of people equal.

He got his green card and citizenship. Then he went back to China and brought my grandmother and my father to America. Later he brought my mother here while she was pregnant with me.

My mom likes it here. She likes how efficient it is. Amazon is her true love. She has Amazon Prime and buys something every week. She's been bugging me recently to go back to China with her during the summer of my senior year. My mom's very good at being cheerful and happy; my dad is more on the quiet side but he can be cheerful and happy too. I'm more like my grandfather; he's kind of cynical and sarcastic, and more realistic.

I consider myself a descendant of immigrants, but not an immigrant. I feel bad for students who are first generation because they have to assimilate—or keep their identity and be considered "unique." I've been called smart. I'm grateful that the Asian stereotype is being smart; it's like being known for being beautiful. How is that a bad thing? People also say I have a voice like a white girl, which I never noticed. Americans try to be open, but whatever's different from our culture makes us want to back away.

Chinese tradition is very different. My grandmother's very old-fashioned. She speaks a lot of Chinese dialects. My grandfather celebrates his parents' and grandparents' death by doing a ritual where they put small red papers with cutout characters on top of food on a table like a giant feast and burn them. It represents bringing food to the ancestors in the afterworld.

In my grandfather's day, Fuzhou, his town, was like a village. They had stick huts. There's still one across from his house. I like the fact that China is a really old country and has a lot of history. We made Confucianism. We've had a lot of education. We are diverse. We have hundreds of dialects and many different tribes. I don't like the government system and the revolution they had after the civil war. I'm not proud of World War II, either, though it wasn't necessarily our fault. And I don't like the smog and the air pollution.

My grandfather and my mother live with me, which I like. It's nice and quiet. My father lives in New York with my grandmother. They all believe in me and want to take care of me.

I'm the only child, so I'm the only hope. But it seems like I'm good at what I do, so I see my future as a one-way street. I'm looking forward to my career as a fine-arts professor, that's what I want. I have no regrets. It doesn't matter if I regret something—that's not going to fix it. I'm alive, I'm doing well.

Trust: ثقة (Arabic) n. to find your way in the darkness with the help of others

When I first came to the United States I had to trust others to help me through the challenges.

Doha, Iraq

I was born in Iraq but then when I was about three years old we moved from Iraq to Syria, and then from Syria we moved to the United States.

I don't remember much about Iraq, just the house that we had where my mom's family was all gathered around, and my father's family's big farm. There was a big lake where we could swim. During the Eid holiday everyone gathered and sat there together. My uncle made a swing for us.

When Iraq was invaded the soldiers came into our house. They came out of nowhere, they broke in. They had helmets on and guns in their hands. I still have nightmares about it.

We were sitting in the living room. We didn't have sofas so we were all sitting on the floor. My mom, my grandma, and aunts were baking, working on a big dough. As soon as I saw the soldiers, my mom dropped her head and wrapped it with her scarf.

The soldiers started looking around. They went to my parents' room. They threw everything around. I don't know if the soldiers were looking for weapons. They even looked in the fridge. The worst part is that my grandfather was out of the house. My dad was out of the house. Only my aunts were there and they didn't know what to do.

I have nightmares that someone will break into our house and ask for our weapons. So when my dad told me that we're going to come to America, I didn't know how we were going to live here. I thought there were going to be soldiers all around.

After the soldiers broke in, my dad said, "I want a safer place for my family," so we moved to Syria. I remember the long car ride from Iraq. It was me, my sister, my younger brother, my mom, my dad—all in that one car, and Syrians as well.

Syrian people do not like Iraqis. They thought we were backwards. They thought we were going to ruin the country for them. They said, "The Iraqis are fleeing their country; we don't really want them here."

My father arranged everything. Our first school was in Syria. I remember my parents walking us to school for the first time. We had to wear uniforms, blue colored dresses with dark-colored pants. There was a big open field, and inside was the school. I wasn't the kind who made friends easily. And because I'm Iraqi, some people would just back away from me. That continued until I came here. Iraqis were my only friends.

My dad didn't have a steady job, so he moved a lot and worked in different places. My mom stayed home with us. My dad applied for immigration to America, because he said it's going to be bigger opportunities for us.

We had interviews. During the interviews they would ask me and my sister questions about our family, where we were going, why we wanted to go. They even had translators because the interviewers spoke in English. They took pictures of us. There was always a big line we had to wait in.

Syria was a nice place, especially the mountains, but a week before we left, a bomb exploded near us. We were all sleeping. We woke up from a big noise. The windows broke. We had a wood-and-coal heater. That heater cracked and the smoke went all over. It was hard to breathe.

Everyone was terrified. Our ceiling caved in; the door was knocked down. My neighbor's father broke his leg. Then everyone was outside and going crazy. My grandmother was sleeping near the window but at midnight she moved away. She would have been cut by the broken glass. That was my last memory of Syria.

My dad called the owner and he fixed the ceiling. We packed, we cleaned everything. We got out before the civil war. My father was afraid that we would miss our plane because they wouldn't let anyone out of the country. They were stopping Iraqis because they blamed them for the bombing.

We had an immigration meeting that same day. We were told someone would be waiting for us in the airport when we got to the United States. My uncle rented a van to take us to the airport. It was seven in the morning.

I was nine then. I was thinking, OK, we're going to get there and then what? Then what? When we got here, my father didn't know where to go so he just followed people who he thought were American. We ended up in New York, JFK. Then we took another plane to Kentucky and that's when we got off. There was a man waiting.

Sometimes I feel even when we didn't have anything in Iraq, we were just so happy because we had each other. Last year it was really hot over there. They sent us pictures sitting in a park, but it wasn't a park, it was like a junkyard. They were all sitting happy with a picnic.

He drove us to our new apartment in Kentucky. It was one in the morning. I remember my mom waking us up. She said we're here. I looked around and saw it's so quiet. It was night so I barely saw anything. But in the morning, my father opened the balcony and fresh air came in and it felt different. We stayed in the house all day because my father was waiting for a lady from Iraq who was a translator. Then we heard someone knock. She'd come to help us.

I was actually calm. It was kind of a happy moment because during that month we were only the third family in that neighborhood who immigrated. People from Burma already lived there. It was really interesting meeting people from different countries, different cultures.

It's easier to become friends with other people from other cultures because I feel they have the same experience. We stayed in Kentucky for a year. My father had a friend in Philadelphia, so we moved here.

Right now my dad works in Drexel food preparation. And my mom works in a warehouse. That was her first job ever working. She works from six in the morning to six in the evening. And sometimes she even takes overtime, on Saturday and Sunday.

I like living here. I would like it much better if I had the rest of my family here or had them around us. My dad applied for a visa for my grandfather. He was accepted, but during his interview he had to go to the hospital. He couldn't finish the interview. They couldn't give him another date. He reapplied to come here with my grandma, my uncle, his wife and his son, my aunt. They were all refused.

Nothing really comes easy. I worry about my family. Sometimes I feel even when we didn't have anything in Iraq, we were just so happy because we had each other. Last year it was really hot over there. They sent us pictures sitting in a park, but it wasn't a park, it was like a junkyard. They were all sitting happy with a picnic. Even though it was hard for them, they found a way.

My Arabic is broken because I speak more English now. And if I went home, whenever Iraqis see you, they say, oh, you're coming from America. You're this rich person that's swimming in gold. Why would you even come back here? Sometimes I get confused. I just don't know who I am honestly.

All through middle school, I faked my personality. I'd try not to talk whenever other people talked about where they were from. I hated talking about being from Iraq, and everyone just looked at me and had this bad idea of me. But now, it's kind of different. I have more friends who have the same experiences as me, so I feel more comfortable being myself.

I honestly like studying, which is weird. I love having a to-do list. If you just give me a job, I'll do it and I'll be happy with it.

I just want to be who I am. I want to help as many people as I can. Especially translating. I think that makes me happy. I always go to Mrs. Salandy (the ESOL teacher) whenever we have new students who need translating. When we were first in school in Kentucky we didn't have someone to translate for us. We had to force ourselves to learn English. I don't want the people who come here to go through that same process. I was quiet for so long because no one understood me, and I wouldn't understand them. Then I started reading more books.

Wearing the hijab makes me feel like I'm showing who I am and what I represent. At first I felt awkward going to school. People didn't really say much about it. But they would glance at me, even once pulling my whole hijab off. But then when I got to this school, people would see me and they would say *As-salamu alaykum* like in our culture. If I didn't wear the hijab I'd have to explain more.

Upset: Molesto (Spanish) adj. the feeling of being down

I feel like it's not other people that make you upset, it's the life you are living.

Amariah, Pakistan

There are a lot of people who come here illegally and *then* they apply. But it took us twelve years to come here legally, so we don't have to deal with all the problems people who come here illegally have. They can't go back.

But I lost good friends and I lost good memories of the land where I was born, where my grandmother died. I used to know everything about my land. I knew the *plug* (the person who knows everything). There were farms all around and fields with a lot of houses joined together to make a community. They grew wheat and fruits—like watermelons and grapes.

We moved to the city when I was two or three years old. But every three months, we went back to visit our village. We had a big house, so all my family stayed together. In Pakistan, you can build any kind of house you want as long as you build it yourself. We stayed there during summer vacation and during Christmas and Easter and other holidays. Everybody there was Christian. I had good friends, and my whole family was there. The neighbors treated us like family. Here you have to call somebody before you go to their house and visit them. There you could visit anybody anytime, stay with them, chill around. They didn't care. We had a really good time.

I was kind of excited to leave Pakistan. All the flights stopped in some country and so Manchester in England was our stop. We had a little stay for eight hours. They had to check the airplane. We got off and they took us to a hotel. They told us you can eat whatever you want. But we didn't know English, so we didn't eat anything.

It was my first time on a plane. My friends told me the plane was going to go up in the air and you're going to die. I said no, that's not going to happen. I was a little nervous but my family was there for me.

Then we got to the USA, to New York. And we drove to Philadelphia for three hours. Ever get lost? It was going to be really difficult if we got lost. I knew where I was going but you're always scared the first time. What if we made a mistake and went somewhere else? We wanted a stable life. We didn't know English. My dad used to be a teacher, so he knew a little bit.

I thought we came to Philadelphia in the USA just for a visit. My family said, no—you're here to stay; this is your new home now. It felt so sad, not to be going back to my country, not being able to see my land. I was twelve years old. I was little but I was mature enough. I'd left my friends and my home but I understood that our parents were here for a better future. I had to think they knew better than me.

There are a lot of Christian people in Pakistan. To me, being Christian is everything. We're different. We always have to stay calm if someone is doing bad to us. My mom gave me a blessing so nothing would happen to me when I left home. There were people who bullied me in school in Pakistan because they were Muslim and I was the only Christian. I felt really sad. Why were they doing this to me? Your religion is something you keep to yourself. It's something you practice for yourself. It's what your family believes.

When I'm home with my family here, or at church and gatherings, I'm in my culture. When I'm outside of home, like at school, I'm in American culture. It's like 50/50 home and school. So I don't forget my culture.

I wasn't hoping to live in the USA. Just getting here was really difficult. A plane ticket cost a hundred thousand rupees. That's a lot of money. And there were five in our family. I don't know how my father arranged it. He didn't tell me. He said he was a teacher, a professor. Now he's a nurse. He studied four years here because his degrees from Pakistan don't count here.

On my fourth day in the USA, my aunt sent me to school. When I got there, I saw people I never knew existed in the world—white people, black people, Spanish people, and Chinese people. We never saw these people in our country. From September until November I didn't speak to anyone in the class. They would just make fun of me. They'd say, what happened to you, you don't have a mouth?

There were a lot of things I had to change to fit in. At home, my father always ate with his hands. I tried that once over here and everybody looked at me like I was stupid.

When it was lunch, I would just eat alone and sit on a bench and sometimes do my homework and like, look around. I saw people playing. I wanted to be like them.

One time a teacher came to our class and said, you've got to write down on a paper what things you're supposed to bring to school. I thought she meant what you were *not* supposed to bring to school. So I wrote guns and knives and things like that.

> *To me, being Christian is everything. We're different. We always have to stay calm if someone is doing bad to us. My mom gave me a blessing so nothing would happen to me when I left home.*

Next day she called me to her office and said, you're from Pakistan. So what are you doing here? I didn't say anything. She said she was going to call the cops, but she had to contact my family first. She called my cousin who knew English and my cousin told her I didn't know English. The teacher told me she was going to give me an ESOL class—a tutor. Then I started learning a bit.

Everything changed since I came here to Northeast High School. Nobody treats you bad, and there are people from other countries that are my friends. Some people are from India or Bangladesh, and they all speak the same language as me—Urdu. Also there is Hindi. We write it our way and they write it their way but the language is the same.

It's been five years since I've been here. I still haven't gone back. It's really bad in Pakistan right now. They don't care if you're Muslim, Christian, or anybody—if you come from America or another rich country, they chase you down and stick you up at gunpoint and take your money. We just heard the latest news in Pakistan. There are four Christians who they're trying to force to become Muslim or they'll kill them.

I'm happy I didn't go back to Pakistan. It's better here. Over there, we couldn't even imagine what we have here. We couldn't afford a phone there. This country is blessed. You can get things easily. I love this country. I like the freedom. Over there, there was no freedom of speech. They would just not listen to you. And they would kill you.

I'm happy that I'm here.

Vv

VISA

VISTO

VISA

UNITED STATES OF AMERICA

Issuing Post Name
SAO PAULO
Surname

Given Name
SUELLEN
Passport Number

Entries
M
Annotation

Control Number

Sex
F

Issue Date
15OCT2015

Birth Date
31MAY2000

Visa Type /Class
R

Expiration Date
07OCT2025

K8066525

SUELLEN<<<<<<<<<<<

ADMITTED
MIA
JUN 25 2016

BZ
DEC 24 2016

Visa: Visto (Portuguese) n. a stamp in your passport that allows you to enter another country

My entire family had to go to the consulate to get a visa. We had to fill out a lot of paperwork. Then they stamped the visas in our passports.

Suellen, Brazil

I had plans, you know, plans for my entire life. I knew where I wanted to go to college in Brazil. I still want to major in journalism. I knew where I wanted to work and I had my friends and my family. My dad had a store. Then our president got impeached and the prices increased so badly that my dad had to close the store. Then he was like, "You know what, I am going to give it a shot. I am going to go to the US and I'm going to see how it works." He rented a house and then my sister and I came here for vacation.

We got a flight from Brazil to Miami. When we first got here, it was so hot. We had to stay in the airport for a long time. I told my sister, "I don't feel like we are in the US." My sister suggested we do something to make it feel like we're in the US. When we were walking in the street I felt like we were still in Brazil. People walking around in bikinis, the weather and the music everywhere. Then we got to a store and it was the first time I ever spoke English with someone. After that I felt like I was in the US.

We had tickets to go back. Three days before our flight, my dad came to me and told me that I was staying here. I thought, "Dude, why are you doing this to me?" I don't know if I am going to be able to do the same things I wanted to do there here. So I felt a little disappointed. But I started to look at things in a positive way. I am going to be able to do new things.

DACA (Deferred Action for Childhood Arrivals) allows me to go to college and actually work here because I am a minor. Technically it wasn't my choice to come here, so I do have rights. But I cannot go to Brazil or somewhere else. I have to choose if I want to stay here for the rest of my life, or if I want to go travel the world and not be able to come back to my family. That's a big problem, unless I marry someone that is American. But what if that doesn't happen? You do not choose who you fall in love with. I am not going to be willing to be one of those people who does it to get a green card.

I said to my parents last week, "You know what, I do not know if I want to stay here. Maybe I want to go to Brazil, maybe I want to go to somewhere in Europe. I do not know if I want to stay here." And my mother said, "That's fine because I understand that you want to do things. You want to travel, but you're not going to see us because we do not plan on going back to Brazil right now."

I don't know if I am being selfish or not because it is my life. I do love my parents and I do love my brothers. My youngest brother is three years old and if I go out of the country next year to college, I'm not going to be able to see him for ten years. That's when you can get a new visa, so it's kind of a tough choice. I don't know what I'm going to do with my life next year.

But whenever I say to my dad, "My friends are planning a trip to Canada, and I can't go because I can't come back," I see in his face that he thinks, "Yeah, that's my fault and I did that to you." But I do not want to put the blame on him.

Water: ماء (Arabic) n. a liquid that the world needs to live

There are people who have to leave their countries because they don't have water. When the sky sees them, it starts crying rain to help them.

Aya, Iraq

I remember the hot sun in Iraq. It was just the desert, the sand. And rocks. That's all. I can't remember so well because I was little. I can remember flashing things.

There are two kinds of Muslim people: Shiite and Sunni. Me and my mom are Sunnis and my dad was Shiite. The Sunnis and Shiites just killed each other like animals. We weren't that kind of people. We don't like fighting, but my dad died.

My mom decided to go to her family in Syria. I was six years old. We went, me and my uncle, my mom, my brother; he was three years old. We started a new life. We were happy until my grandma and my big uncle with his family went to America. I was twelve and the war started in Syria. Another uncle, who has four boys and one girl, they decided to go to Turkey. We went to Jordan to a new place away from the war, to make a new life. We lived for one year in Jordan. One uncle was still in Syria; frightened by the war, he would talk to us every day and then in 2016 he went to Canada. We came to America.

Now I've spent just one year with all my family together here, except my one uncle in Canada. Every weekend another uncle comes from New York to visit us and we have a party. We go to the parking lot to barbecue and we're happy all together. But now we're scared of the new president. Is he going to have another war? I'm sad. I don't want to go to another place.

I hope we're going to stay all together and nothing happens again. I like to work hard. I like to feel I am doing something. I'd love to do something to help other people. I feel for everyone who needs help and is sad. I'd like to help my family and I'd like to help myself.

X, x

Not A Letter In Bengali Turkish Urdu Arabic

X: the 24th letter of the English alphabet, a consonant

The letter X is not a letter in Turkish, Urdu, Bengali, or Arabic—languages that many immigrants speak.

Youth: Thiếu niên (Vietnamese) n. the next generation of young people full of aspirations and expected to pursue their dreams

My youth will be spent working hard in school so that I can graduate from school and show that being an immigrant is not a disadvantage.

Kayla, Puerto Rico

I think immigrants bring something to America: a new outlook on the world. Here in America we want everything to be a certain way, and immigrants bring in new ways to look at things and do things.

I don't think of myself as an immigrant. My father is from here, from Philly. My mother understands Spanish, but she doesn't speak it.

My mom used to make beef patties. I realized when I was around four or five that she was from another culture. I asked my parents one day what race I was. Since I went to a mostly African American school, some kids thought I looked a little different. They would ask me if I was mixed with another race. I actually liked it because I felt different from everybody. It made me think about my background, where I came from, and ever since then I've felt like learning about my family history. It could help define me. I'm not just American.

I have one close friend, Gaby. She's from Guyana. We do a lot of stuff together, like drawing and basketball and dancing. Gaby's somebody I can open up to and really talk to. A little while ago, we joined a multicultural dance group. As we danced we got to know each other's cultures and I've gotten to know Gaby's culture. It's nice to know new things.

My grandmother came from Ponce with my grandpa, but I never got to meet him. They split up, and now my grandpa lives in New York. When I was younger, my grandmother used to speak Spanish with me. But as I got older, we grew distant and I lost the language.

My grandmother's name is Miriam. She lives in Philadelphia. My other two uncles live in New York. I've never been there. My aunt travels back and forth to Puerto Rico. I'd like to go see it. I think it's warm and sunny and there would be a lot more culture than we see around here because it would be more focused on Hispanic culture.

I like hearing other people's stories. I think it's inspiring that other students actually know the histories and journeys of where their ancestors came from. I'd like to know that.

Zero: صِفر (Arabic) n. a number that represents nothing
Every immigrant starts their journey from zero.

I'd like to thank Hazami Sayed for her dedication to young immigrants in Philadelphia and her celebration, through art and culture, of the countries they came from. I'm grateful for her invitation to work with an astounding group of high school students who—despite sadness and difficulties—openly shared their stories. Thank you from my heart—Amariah, Aya, Doha, Duvelt, Gabriel, Gabrielle, George, Jenny, Joseph, Kazi, Kayla, Malika, Marian, Rushana, Salawat, Suellen, Tania, and Xuan.

This book was conceived as a public art installation produced by Al-Bustan Seeds of Culture. Pete Mauney, Nora Elmarzouky, Diana Misdary, Megan Madison, and the staff of Al-Bustan Seeds of Culture helped us bring the project to life. Jeff Hirsch at Fotocare and Jeff Whetstone generously provided the photographic equipment we needed. Linda Carroll, Sharon McCloskey, and Margaret De Naples, and the rest of the faculty at Northeast High School, particularly Sonia Salandy and Jay Fluellen, made it possible for us to work comfortably with the students.

Thanks to my agent, Chuck Verrill, and editor, Megan Tingley; to Anna Prendella and Sasha Illingworth at Little, Brown; and to Paloma Dooley, my assistant, who all made this book possible. As always I must thank my husband, Tom McDonough, for his faith in this project and his help in editing.

This book was edited by Megan Tingley and Anna Prendella and designed by Sasha Illingworth and Angela Taldone. The production was supervised by Erika Schwartz, and the production editor was Annie McDonnell. The text was set in Adobe Garamond Pro, and the display type is Agfa Rotis Sans Serif.

The photographs in this book were taken using a Hasselblad H5D-50c, a medium-format digital camera, and two lenses: 80mm and 120mm. We set up a portrait studio with lights and backdrops that were changed according to the students' preferences. I worked with the students in pairs alongside my assistant Pete Mauney and Nora Elmarzouky, the former Director of Education at Al-Bustan Seeds of Culture, to set up the shots, draw on the images, and write the sentences and definitions. The students drew the letters and words of the alphabet with colored Sharpies on transparency material. Then we scanned the transparencies and layered the scans with the photographic files in Photoshop.

Since the students worked in pairs or sometimes in threes, the students in the photographs are not always the students interviewed. The students also created journey maps that depicted the routes from their countries of origin to Philadelphia, and some of the illustrations from Jenny's map appear throughout the book.